MICROBITES
DINOSAURS
RIVETING READS FOR CURIOUS KIDS

M I C R O B I T E S
DINOSAURS
RIVETING READS FOR CURIOUS KIDS

By
Dougal Dixon

Consultants
David Lambert
Chris Barker

Revised Edition

DK Delhi

Project Editor Neha Ruth Samuel
Project Art Editor Mansi Agrawal
Editorial team Virien Chopra,
Sukriti Kapoor
Art Editor Sanya Jain
Managing Editor Kingshuk Ghoshal
Managing Art Editor Govind Mittal
Senior DTP Designer Shanker Prasad
DTP Designers Mohammad Rizwan,
Mrinmoy Mazumdar
Pre-Production Manager Balwant Singh
Production Manager Pankaj Sharma

DK London

Senior Editor Shaila Brown
Project Editor Amanda Wyatt
US Editor Kayla Dugger
US Executive Editor Lori Cates Hand
Managing Editor Lisa Gillespie
Managing Art Editor Owen Peyton Jones
Production Editor Gillian Reid
Senior Production Controller Meskerem Berhane
Jacket Designer Akiko Kato
Jacket Design Development Manager Sophia MTT
Publisher Andrew Macintyre
Associate Publishing Director Liz Wheeler
Art Director Karen Self
Publishing Director Jonathan Metcalf

First Edition

Project Editor Steve Setford
Project Art Editor Peter Radcliffe
Senior Editor Fran Jones
Senior Art Editor Marcus James
Category Publisher Jayne Parsons
Managing Art Editor Jacquie Gulliver
Picture Researcher Sean Hunter
Production Erica Rosen
DTP Designers Matthew Ibbotson, Louise Paddick

This American Edition, 2020
First American Edition, 2001
Published in the United States by DK Publishing
1450 Broadway, Suite 801, New York, NY 10018

Copyright © 2001, 2020 Dorling Kindersley Limited
DK, a Division of Penguin Random House LLC
20 21 22 23 24 10 9 8 7 6 5 4 3 2 1
001–318200–Jun/2020

A catalog record for this book is available from the Library of Congress.
ISBN 978-1-4654-9736-9 (Paperback)
ISBN 978-1-4654-9845-8 (Hardcover)

DK books are available at special discounts when purchased in bulk
for sales promotions, premiums, fund-raising, or educational use.
For details, contact: DK Publishing Special Markets,
1450 Broadway, Suite 801, New York, NY 10018
SpecialSales@dk.com

Printed and bound in the UK

For the curious

www.dk.com

CONTENTS

INTRODUCTION

Dinosaurs! We see their skeletons in museums, photographs of them in books, and images of them in films and on television. But what were these amazing creatures that have so caught our imagination? And how do we know so much about them?

The name dinosaur means "terrible lizard." These creatures were land-living reptiles that dominated life on Earth around 240 to 66 million years ago, during the Mesozoic Era. The Mesozoic is often referred to as the Age of Reptiles. Scientists have divided this part of history into three periods of time—the Triassic, the Jurassic, and the Cretaceous. You'll learn more about the world during these periods as you read this book.

Nobody knew anything about dinosaurs until about 200 years ago. Ancient peoples saw dinosaur fossils in the rocks, but they did not understand what they were. After all, if you knew nothing about dinosaurs and discovered a limb bone that was as long as you are, what would you make of it—a giant or a dragon perhaps?

PACHYCEPHALOSAURUS WAS A DINOSAUR THAT LIVED ABOUT 70 MILLION YEARS AGO, IN THE LATE CRETACEOUS. IT ATE FRUITS AND LEAVES.

The first remains to be studied properly were found in England in the early 19th century. Soon, discoveries were being made in mainland Europe and in North America as well. Since then, dinosaur remains have been found on every continent, with the first Antarctic discoveries occurring during the 1980s.

Over the past two centuries, paleontologists (fossil experts) and other scientists have been drawing together all the evidence. Now we think we have a good idea of what dinosaurs were and how they lived. But new discoveries often turn established ideas on their heads, so welcome to the ever-changing world of dinosaurs!

DINO SPOTTING

You stand in an ancient forest, with unfamiliar conifer trees towering over you, the ferny undergrowth tickling your legs, and strange insects buzzing around you in the heat. In front of you, in the shade of a tree, is an animal you have never seen before. It is about your size and is standing on its hind legs. It is a dinosaur!

Plant or meat eater?

What kind of dinosaur is it? As you mentally flip through all your dinosaur books, some of the names come back to you. Meat-eating *Deinonychus* and *Ornitholestes*, plant-eating *Hypsilophodon* and *Stegoceras*— all are about the same size and walk on their hind legs. But is this one a plant eater, or is it a meat eater? If it likes to feed on leaves, shoots, and other vegetation, it will probably not bother you if you keep your distance; if it prefers a nice big juicy steak, you are in deep trouble! The dinosaur is staring at you, so you need to find out quickly. But first, you will need to check out a few things.

1. How is it standing? All meat eaters—the dinosaurs in the group scientists call the theropods—walked on their hind legs, using their tails for balance. But that doesn't help you much. Many members of the major plant-eating dinosaur groups, including the ornithopods, could also move around on two legs.

2. Look at its jaws and teeth. If it has sharp teeth and curved claws on its hand, it's more likely to be a meat eater. If it has a beak at the front and "cheeks" on the side, it's probably a plant eater. But with its head turned toward you, it may be difficult to tell.

WEIRD WORLD

MODERN-DAY BIRDS ARE SURVIVING DINOSAURS. MANY DINOSAURS THAT LIVED DURING THE MESOZOIC ERA FALL OUTSIDE THE BIRD GROUP IN THE DINOSAUR FAMILY TREE AND ARE REFERRED TO AS "NONBIRD" DINOSAURS.

AN *IGUANODON*—A TYPE OF ORNITHOPOD—
IN A GLOOMY FOREST WOULD MAKE
ANYONE STOP AND LOOK. AT FIRST
GLANCE, HOWEVER, IT WOULD BE
DIFFICULT TO TELL WHETHER
THIS ANIMAL WAS
DANGEROUS
OR NOT.

BRACHYLOPHOSAURUS HAD A BEAK (FOR CUTTING UP PLANTS), GRINDING TEETH BEHIND, AND STRONG JAW MUSCLES. IT HAD "CHEEK" POUCHES AT THE SIDE SO IT COULD CHEW GREAT MOUTHFULS OF PLANTS.

3. The body size could be a giveaway. Often, plant eaters would be larger than meat eaters with wider guts to help them digest the tough plants they fed on.

4. Does it have feathers? Many of the theropods, which are the cousins of modern birds, were covered in feathers. However, not all feathered theropods were meat eaters. In addition, feathers may have evolved in creatures before the dinosaurs, and some nontheropod dinosaurs were feathered, too!

A dangerous situation
With all this knowledge, you should be able to tell what kind of dinosaur faces you. But then what do you do? A plant eater will probably just move away or ignore you. But if it is a meat eater, you could be in great danger—it might attack you. You've probably heard that a meat-eating dinosaur's eyes work on movement, so if its would-be prey stands still, it can't detect it. Don't believe a word of this!

LONG-NECKED, PLANT-EATING GIRAFFATITAN MAY HAVE STRIPPED LEAVES OFF TREES WITH ITS SMALL TEETH.

MEAT-EATING *ALBERTOSAURUS* HAD SHARP RIPPING TEETH, ALL DIFFERENT SIZES AND SERRATED LIKE STEAK KNIVES. THE JAW WAS HINGED FOR CHOMPING FOOD RATHER THAN CHEWING IT.

Meat-eating theropods had keen senses and may well have had good vision. Some species probably had an excellent sense of smell. So standing still is no surefire way of keeping safe, and the predator is likely to be aware of your presence. The problem is that, although we can identify it as a meat-eating dinosaur, we don't know enough about its habits to anticipate how it might attack. From here, you are on your own—so good luck!

Cut it up

Of course, you'd get a better idea of what kind of animal you had if it lay dead at your feet. You then could see its jaws and teeth. If you could look inside it, what you would find would be even more interesting. Cut open the belly of the dinosaur. (You wouldn't dare set off exploring in the Mesozoic Era without at least a penknife.) The guts spill out. Cover your nose to avoid the stench, and use a fern frond to sweep away the flies that gather on the gooey mess. Yes, flies have evolved by

SPINOSAURUS, A MEAT EATER, HAD RIDGED TEETH, WHICH MAY HAVE HELPED IT GRIP SLIPPERY PREY SUCH AS FISH.

this point in the Mesozoic, and they are just as irritating and obnoxious as they are today!

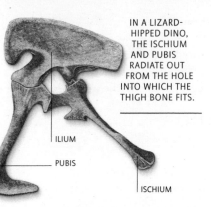

IN A LIZARD-HIPPED DINO, THE ISCHIUM AND PUBIS RADIATE OUT FROM THE HOLE INTO WHICH THE THIGH BONE FITS.

ILIUM

PUBIS

ISCHIUM

Inside a dinosaur

Rummaging through the innards, you'll probably find a four-chambered heart within the rib cage. The birds and the living cousins of dinosaurs— the crocodilians—have a four-chambered heart, and it's likely dinosaurs shared this feature, too. In some dinosaurs, such as the theropods or the long-necked plant eaters called the sauropods, the lungs

which would have helped clean the blood of any toxins the dinosaur might have picked up

INTESTINES   ILIUM

ISCHIUM

THIS IS WHAT WE MIGHT HAVE FOUND INSIDE A PLANT-EATING DINOSAUR SUCH AS *IGUANODON*.

probably had extensions, just like a bird. This helped them take in more oxygen and made their skeleton lighter. The digestive system of meat eaters and plant eaters possibly differed, too. In meat eaters, the intestines may have been shorter and the liver larger, from the meat. In plant eaters, the intestines were probably very long, as vegetation is tricky to break down and needs a lot of time in the gut.

The telltale hips

If you are still up for it, keep cutting away the flesh beneath the legs until you find the hip bones. In most theropod meat eaters, the hip bones are arranged like those of lizards, with the pubis, one of the two lower hip bones, pointing forward and the other, the ischium, pointing backward. An ornithopod plant eater

IN BIRD-HIPPED DINOSAURS, EACH HIP CONSISTED OF A FLAT ILIUM BONE AT THE TOP AND SWEPT-BACK ISCHIUM AND PUBIS BONES.

ILIUM

ISCHIUM

PUBIS

has hips like those of a bird, with both the pubis and the ischium swept backward out of the way. This may have changed the way these plant eaters breathed in and out.

LUNG

HEART

STOMACH

Out come the scavengers

But now it's time to make a rapid exit. The smells of meat and death have alerted all the scavenging animals in the area, which start to converge on the corpse. The body is torn to pieces. Flesh and organs are eaten, and the bones are carried off. The remains rot away into the soil. After a few days, there is nothing left but a stain on the ground. Nothing left to fossilize. No wonder we still don't know and may never know about every dinosaur that ever existed.

HOW FOSSILS FORM

So how on earth did any dinosaur ever manage to become fossilized? Let's imagine a *Corythosaurus*, a plant eater living on the wooded lowlands of what is now western North America 75 million years ago. Our dinosaur has died relatively young—times were hard and dangerous during the Mesozoic, and rarely did dinosaurs reach old age.

Death of a dinosaur
The *Corythosaurus* is one of several gathered by a lowland stream. The dinosaur is frail and vulnerable to disease. As it crouches on the bank to take a drink, the great effort of lowering its head to the water proves too much for it. Disease finally takes its toll—the blood supply to its little brain fails

CORYTHOSAURUS HAD A NARROW, CURVED BEAK FOR STRIPPING LEAVES OFF PLANTS AND A DISTINCTIVE CREST ON ITS HEAD. IT TRAVELED IN LARGE HERDS THROUGH PLAINS, FORESTS, AND SWAMPS.

and life withdraws from its weary body. With a final gasp, it collapses in a lifeless heap at the water's edge.

Corpse on the move

For days, the rain has been falling in the mountains, and now the lowland stream is becoming swollen with mountain floodwater. The muddy torrent sweeps around the body of the *Corythosaurus*, gathers it up, and washes it downstream. Some distance away, the current slows and the heaviest of the flood debris begins to settle. The waters fall back to their normal level, and the corpse is left high and dry in the sun.

Laid to rest

As the carcass rots, bacteria break down the internal organs, and the gases they produce cause the bloated carcass to break open. Insects join the fray, colonizing the remains until it is teeming with maggots and larvae. Later, in the next flood, the waters swirl around the body again. By now the tendons have rotted, the flesh has fallen away, and the skeleton has begun to break up. The skull, a lightweight jigsaw puzzle of interlocked bones, collapses. A large chunk of the tail breaks off and washes away, as do some of the "fingers" of the forelimbs. Luckily, before

A DEAD DINOSAUR FALLING INTO A RIVER COULD SINK AND BE COVERED WITH SEDIMENT, SUCH AS SAND, SILT, OR MUD, INCREASING ITS CHANCES OF BECOMING A FOSSIL.

the skeleton is destroyed completely, the receding floodwater deposits a thick layer of sediment (mostly river sand) over the *Corythosaurus*.

It remains safely buried for a long, long, long time. What you've just read represents the "taphonomy" of the dinosaur. To save you from running for the dictionary, that's the word for the study of what happens to the body of an animal after it dies and before the body becomes fossilized. The technical term for what happens next in the fossilizing process is actually "diagenesis"— but to keep things simple, we'll just call it …

WEIRD WORLD

THE EARTH ROTATED FASTER IN DINOSAUR TIMES. BECAUSE OF THIS, DAYS WERE SHORTER AND THERE WERE 380 DAYS IN A YEAR, NOT 365 AS THERE ARE TODAY.

Turning to stone

Because the flat river plain where *Corythosaurus* died floods frequently, the skeleton soon becomes entombed by layer upon layer of sediment.

Eventually, the land sinks beneath the sea, and marine sediments—including the remains of dead sea creatures—are laid down upon it. As millions of years pass, spaces between them become smaller and smaller. Water trickling down through the sediment layers deposits minerals between the sand particles, gluing them together to form hard sandstone rock. Meanwhile,

IT'S POSSIBLE ONLY ONE DINOSAUR IN A MILLION WAS FOSSILIZED

the weight of all the sediment layers above squeezes the river sand around our *Corythosaurus* skeleton. The sand particles are squashed together so that the minerals that originally made up the dinosaur's bones are slowly replaced molecule by molecule by new minerals, turning the bones into stone.

THIS FOSSIL FORMED FROM THE BODY OF AN *EDMONTOSAURUS* THAT DRIED AND SHRIVELED BEFORE BEING QUICKLY BURIED.

BONY TENDONS HELPED
KEEP THE TAIL RIGID.

Burial or destruction

The process is now complete—
our *Corythosaurus* skeleton has
become a fossil. Sealed in
rock underground, it is likely
to remain there forever,
unseen by human eyes.
Unless, that is, the rock
containing the skeleton
is thrust up toward
the surface when the
huge plates that make
up the Earth's crust
crunch together
and throw up
great mountain
ranges. Even
then, there
is only a slim
chance that our

LARGE BONES WERE
MORE LIKELY TO
FOSSILIZE THAN
SMALLER ONES.

FINDING DINO FOSSILS TAKES A TRAINED
EYE. USUALLY THE FIND CONSISTS OF
A SINGLE BONE OR PART OF A BONE,
NOT A COMPLETE SKELETON LIKE
THIS *CORYTHOSAURUS*.

IT IS NOT VERY OFTEN THAT A FOSSIL SKELETON IS AS COMPLETE AS THIS. THE LIGHT-SHADED AREAS ARE THE ONLY PARTS OF THIS *CORYTHOSAURUS* SKELETON THAT WERE MISSING.

DINOSAUR SKULLS WERE MADE UP OF MANY BONES, SOME OF WHICH WERE FUSED TOGETHER. THIS MIGHT HAVE HELPED KEEP THEM IN PLACE.

SMALL HAND BONES WERE OFTEN WASHED AWAY OR GOT EATEN BY SCAVENGERS.

Corythosaurus skeleton will ever be found. Rain, wind, and frost soon begin to wear down the mountains, breaking up the mountain rocks and any fossils they contain and grinding them into tiny fragments that are washed away.

Discovery

Sadly, that will be the fate of our *Corythosaurus* skeleton. The only hope is that someone passes by at just the right time—as a fossil bone is starting to emerge from the rock—and is sharp-eyed enough to realize what it is. If that person alerts a museum about the discovery, the fossil stands a good chance of being excavated and preserved. So

you can see how heavily the odds are stacked against any dinosaur getting fossilized and any fossils being discovered. We should consider ourselves lucky to have found any at all!

WEIRD WORLD

SCIENTISTS THINK THERE MAY HAVE BEEN 2,000 DIFFERENT NONBIRD DINOSAURS. TO DATE WE ONLY KNOW ABOUT 700 OF THEM BUT WITH INTEREST IN PALEONTOLOGY RISING GLOBALLY, OUR KNOWLEDGE OF THESE FASCINATING CREATURES IS GROWING BY LEAPS AND BOUNDS.

THE DINOSAUR REVEALED

Imagine that you have discovered a dinosaur skeleton—a *Corythosaurus* or a *Tyrannosaurus*—in sandstone rock. You will need to dig it out, but excavation takes a long time. The bones must be removed without breaking them and then transported to a place where they can be studied—a museum or a laboratory in a university.

Protecting the bones

Although the bones have been fossilized, they are still very brittle. They must be protected while they are dug out and removed. Plaster-soaked sacking is best for this. Once you have chiseled away the overlying rock, you must cover the exposed surface of the fossil in this material. Next, you and your team— it's too big a job to tackle on your own—remove each bone or part of the skeleton completely from the rock, turn it over, and encase the rest of it in plaster. At every stage, you photograph what you are doing to keep a record of where it all came from.

Back at the laboratory, you must take off the plaster to allow skilled technicians (called preparators) to remove any remaining rock and to treat the fossil so that it does not decay. Now you can devote yourself to

AFTER DIGGING A TRENCH AROUND A BONE, PALEONTOLOGISTS COAT IT IN SACKING AND RUNNY PLASTER.

A MOUNTED SKELETON, SUCH AS THIS *TYRANNOSAURUS*, IS USUALLY MADE OF CASTS OF THE BONES—NOT THE FOSSILS THEMSELVES.

WEIRD WORLD
A FOSSILIZED DINOSAUR PROTECTED FOR TRAVEL MAY WEIGH SEVERAL TONS (TONNES). IT USUALLY TAKES A HEAVY ALL-TERRAIN VEHICLE OR EVEN A HELICOPTER TO TAKE IT AWAY FROM ITS PLACE OF DISCOVERY.

rebuilding the dinosaur so that you can see what the animal was like when it was alive.

Identification

But what type of dinosaur is it? The experts are quick to tell you that your skeleton is of a *Tyrannosaurus*. Although the ribs, the arms, most of one leg, and pieces of the skull have disappeared, your skeleton is still relatively complete. About 80 percent of the bones are present— more than we get with most dinosaur skeletons. About 50 *Tyrannosaurus* skeletons have been found since the first one was unearthed and named by Americans Henry Fairfield Osborn, a paleontologist, and Barnum Brown, a dinosaur hunter, back in 1905. So a skeleton as complete as the one you found is easy to identify.

21

THIS *TYRANNOSAURUS* LEG SKELETON SHOWS THE MARKS WHERE THE MUSCLES WERE ONCE ATTACHED.

Dino display

If you want to put your *Tyrannosaurus* on public display in a museum, you must first decide whether to build up the skeleton with the actual fossils or with casts of them. Nowadays, it is so easy to make good casts of fossil bones from lightweight materials, such as glass fiber, that this is what is usually done. It makes the display easier to build and keeps the original fossils safe for scientific study. But what about any missing parts of the skeleton? Easy—you speak to the owners of the other 50 or so *Tyrannosaurus* skeletons and arrange to make casts of the bones missing from your own *Tyrannosaurus* skeleton.

Reconstructing and restoring

At last, you have your mounted skeleton for display to the public. This is what is known as a reconstruction. Now you want to build up a picture of what the animal was like when it was alive. A painting, sculpture, or video presentation that shows what the animal was like in life is known as a restoration.

A COMPLETE DINOSAUR SKULL, SUCH AS THIS ONE FROM *TYRANNOSAURUS*, IS A RARE FIND. MOST SKULLS FELL APART BEFORE THEY COULD GET FOSSILIZED.

The two terms are often confused. Be careful with the skull. Like most dinosaur skulls, that of *Tyrannosaurus* consists of struts of bone, so it is full of holes.

There are marks on them that show where the muscles were attached. You can compare these with the marks on the bones of today's animals. From

"FOSSIL" COMES FROM THE LATIN FOR "DUG UP"

In 1920, one of the most famous dinosaur artists of all time, the American Charles R. Knight, painted a *Tyrannosaurus* with its eye in the wrong skull hole. Few people noticed the mistake. The painting was later used as the inspiration for the *Tyrannosaurus* that appeared in the hugely successful 1933 film *King Kong*. So Knight's error went down in movie history.

The muscles
The first step in creating our restoration is to take a close look at the individual bones.

a calculation of the size and weight of the *Tyrannosaurus* and of the force needed to move its limbs, you can work out the size of the muscles it needed. Once you have fleshed out the entire skeleton, you will have a good idea of the shape of the living animal.

23

The skin

All animals are covered with skin. The dinosaurs were, too. Unfortunately, skin is too soft to be easily preserved, so it is rare to find it as a fossil. But now and again, there is a lucky occurrence where a dinosaur has rolled in mud, leaving the impression of its skin behind.

THIS IMPRESSION OF *CORYTHOSAURUS* SKIN SHOWS THAT THE ANIMAL WAS COVERED IN SMALL, BUMPY SCALES.

The impression was preserved when the mud eventually turned to rock (remember the word diagenesis?), leaving us a fossil of the dinosaur's skin texture. There is a skin impression from South America of a big meat-eating dinosaur— not *Tyrannosaurus*, but one slightly smaller in size. This is the closest that we are likely to get, so we can use this skin impression to give us an idea of the surface texture of our animal.

The texture of the bones of the face might give us clues as to the type of tissues covering them, which can be compared

WEIRD WORLD

ONE PARTICULARLY WELL-PRESERVED *TYRANNOSAURUS* SKELETON TOOK FIVE PEOPLE 3 YEARS TO CLEAN AND PREPARE BEFORE IT COULD BE MOUNTED— A TOTAL OF ABOUT 30,000 HOURS OF HARD WORK!

to modern-day animals. Rough, knobby bone texture in some modern animals often has a tough skin overlying it, for instance.

The color

Finally, we must determine the color of the dinosaur. It is one of the first things to change as the animal dies and is hardly ever preserved in the fossil record. However, new finds and powerful imaging techniques have helped discover rare cases of pigment preservation.

The tiny theropod *Microraptor* appears to have had iridescent feathers similar to modern-day starlings. Meanwhile, the spiky, tanklike *Borealopelta* was a rusty red color with a pale underbelly, which seems to be a form of camouflage. This suggests that even these well-armored dinosaurs needed to avoid the attention of hungry meat eaters. *Borealopelta*'s huge shoulder spikes, however, were a lighter color and stood out from the rest of the armor. This may have been used to attract a mate.

MICRORAPTOR HAD SHINY BLACK FEATHERS THAT MAY HAVE HELPED THE DINOSAUR IMPRESS POTENTIAL MATES.

PALEONTOLOGISTS THINK THAT THIS *BOREALOPELTA*'S REMAINS WERE PROBABLY SWEPT INTO THE OCEAN, WHERE IT SANK BACK-FIRST INTO THE SOFT MUD AT THE BOTTOM. THIS HELPED PRESERVE THE FEATURES OF ITS ARMOR.

DINOS GALORE!

Paleontologists have been discovering, excavating, reconstructing, and restoring dinosaurs for almost 180 years, so today we have a good idea of the range of dinosaurs that existed. We can divide the dinosaurs into two major groups, according to the arrangement of their hip bones. One group had lizardlike hips, while the other group had hips that resembled those of a bird.

BARYONYX, A FISH-EATING THEROPOD, HAD ELONGATED JAWS. IT WAS ABOUT 28 FT (8.5 M) LONG AND 10 FT (3 M) TALL.

Lizard-hipped dinos

Most meat-eating dinosaurs had lizardlike hips. The meat eaters are known as theropods, a name that means "beast-footed." The 19th-century scientist who first used this name for meat-eating dinosaurs assumed that they were predators because they had big, sharp, hooked claws on their toes. He noticed that most plant eaters had only blunt "hooves" or toe bones.

Theropod dinosaurs had strong hind legs and long jaws bearing sharp teeth.

But there was incredible variation among the dinosaurs of the theropod group.

Theropod parade

Some theropods were big and powerful, like *Tyrannosaurus*. Others were small and graceful, like the chicken-sized *Compsognathus*. In between was a vast range of dinosaurs, hunting all types of animals and using a range of strategies. There were the dromaeosaurids, fast hunters that used a sickle-shaped claw on the

WITH ITS NECK HELD UP HIGH, THE OSTRICHLIKE *GALLIMIMUS* COULD SWIVEL ITS HEAD AND SEE IN ALL DIRECTIONS.

hind foot to pin down their prey before tearing into them with their teeth. The dromaeosaurids included the goose-sized *Bambiraptor*, the dog-sized *Velociraptor*, the tiger-sized *Deinonychus*, and the even larger *Utahraptor*. There were also fast sprinters, such as *Ornithomimus* and *Gallimimus*, that resembled ostriches. There was also a group of long-snouted theropods called spinosaurs that appeared to have fed on a variety of prey, including fish. The spinosaurs included *Baryonyx* and *Suchomimus*. Some of the earliest known dinosaurs, such as *Herrerasaurus* and *Eoraptor*, share traits with the theropods, but their position in the dinosaur family tree is uncertain and often debated.

The sauropods

The lizard-hipped dinosaurs also included huge, long-necked dinos called sauropods, which means "lizard-footed."

The sauropods had an enormous gut, which they needed to digest the vast

27

quantities of plant food they ate. Small heads lined with simple teeth were perched on elongated necks that helped these dinosaurs reach the leafy treetops. Their bones were hollow, like theropods, and they most likely had birdlike air sacs and efficient lungs to help supply their tissues with plenty of oxygen.

BRACHIOSAURUS MAY HAVE BEEN AS TALL AS A FOUR-STORY BUILDING. OTHER SAUROPODS, INCLUDING *SAUROPOSEIDON*, WERE EVEN LARGER.

Prototype sauropods

The "prosauropods" were an earlier group of lizard-hipped dinos that were once thought to eat both meat and plants. Today, scientists think that they were plant eaters. Many were bipedal, like the theropods, but several types evolved to be four-footed before the evolution of the first true sauropods.

Familiar faces

The most familiar sauropods were the long, low ones like *Diplodocus* and *Barosaurus* and the tall, high-shouldered types

dinosaur era, being particularly widespread in South America. Some titanosaurs, such as *Saltasaurus*, had backs covered in bony armor, which may have helped protect juveniles from predators. The titanosaurs included some of the largest animals to ever walk on Earth— *Argentinosaurus* was probably the largest and may have weighed 88 tons (80 tonnes).

Bird-hipped dinos

Like the sauropods, walking on all four limbs evolved at least three times in the bird-hipped

A YOUNG *DIPLODOCUS* HAD A SKULL THAT MEASURED 9.4 IN (24 CM) LONG

like *Brachiosaurus* and *Sauroposeidon*. One group of sauropods, the titanosaurs, survived until the end of the

dinosaurs, with the horned ceratopsians, armored thyreophorans, and some of the ornithopods all descending from two-legged ancestors. Ornithopod means "bird-footed"—their three-toed feet resembled those of birds.

The largest ornithopods—animals such as *Iguanodon*, *Hadrosaurus*, and *Corythosaurus*—probably spent most of their lives on all fours because of the sheer weight of their bodies. In fact, modern studies show that their front feet were pawlike and built for taking weight. Some of the cousins of the ornithopods, such as *Hypsilophodon*, were built for two-footed speed.

WEIRD WORLD
DINOSAURS IN ONE ORNITHOPOD GROUP, CALLED THE HADROSAURS, HAD MORE THAN 1,000 TEETH IN THEIR JAWS TO HELP GRIND TOUGH PLANTS.

HYPSILOPHODON WAS A SMALL PLANT EATER THAT SCURRIED AROUND THE LUSH FORESTS OF WHAT IS NOW EUROPE IN THE EARLY CRETACEOUS.

The ornithopods were extremely successful during the Cretaceous Period, exploiting a range of new vegetation and evolving the most complex set of teeth of any animal.

The stegosaurs
Another group of bird-hipped dinos was the stegosaurs. Also known as plated dinosaurs, these were among the most flamboyant of the plant eaters,

29

with a double row of plates or spikes running along the back. The function of these extravagant bony structures isn't clear. They probably had

hands were arranged in a tubelike fashion similar to those of sauropods. This helped each hand support the weight of the dinosaur.

THERE WERE MANY MORE PLANT EATERS THAN MEAT EATERS

a tough keratin-rich covering, and the tail spikes may have been used in defense against predators. However, those along the back were too high up to be of much defensive use, and many paleontologists suggest these may have evolved as part of some sort of visual display.

Stegosaurs were plant eaters and moved around on all fours. The bones of their

The ankylosaurs
The highly armored ankylosaurs were related to the stegosaurs. These bird-

hipped dinos had bone embedded in the thick, leathery skin of the head, neck, body, and tail. Some of these tough dinos were so heavily defended that even the eyelids were armored, slamming shut like the steel shutters of a battleship when danger approached.

Spikes and clubs

There were two main groups of ankylosaurs. The first, including *Edmontonia*, had spikes and blades along the sides of the body and tail. These spikes were bigger in the shoulder and neck region and were possibly used as display or to attract mates.

The second group is typified by *Ankylosaurus*, which had a bony club on the end of its tail. The bones in the rear half of the tail were fused, making the tail stiff and strong, like the shaft of a medieval mace. This enabled the bony club

MANY FOUR-FOOTED, BIRD-HIPPED DINOS, SUCH AS *STEGOSAURUS*, HAD SOME FORM OF ARMOR.

to be swung with great force to deliver a mighty whack to the flanks and legs of an attacking theropod. Although known from early Jurassic times, it was in the Cretaceous Period that the ankylosaurs really became common, taking the place of the stegosaurs that had by then begun to die away.

The ceratopsians
The Jurassic saw the development of another group of bird-hipped dinosaurs, called ceratopsians. The ceratopsians evolved from two-footed dinosaurs. One of the earliest examples was

EUOPLOCEPHALUS AND OTHER LARGE ANKYLOSAURS WERE SO HEAVILY ARMORED THAT THEY WERE LIKE WALKING TANKS.

THE EARLIEST CERATOPSIANS, SUCH AS THE PARROTLIKE *PSITTACOSAURUS*, HAD VERY LITTLE ARMOR ON THEIR HEAD.

Psittacosaurus, which had a big beak, giving it a parrotlike appearance. It also had big cheek horns that were probably used for display. By the late Cretaceous Period, some ceratopsians had evolved to form armored neck frills that may have helped them attract mates. The later ceratopsians were divided into two groups— those, such as *Styracosaurus*, that had a large nose horn and a short frill, and those, such as *Triceratops*, that had large brow horns, as well as a nose horn and a long frill.

The bone-heads

Closely related to ceratopsians were the pachycephalosaurs, which included *Stegoceras* and *Pachycephalosaurus*. What made these two-footed plant eaters different was the solid mass of bone on top of their head. This bone dome might have been used as a battering ram or against rivals within the herd. Did this head-banging give them splitting headaches? We'll never know for sure, but probably not, because the bones of their skulls could be up to 10 in (25 cm) thick.

LIFESTYLE CLUES

Now you have the mounted reconstruction of the dinosaur, and you have the restoration that shows what it looked like in life. But that is only part of the story. You need other evidence to tell you how your dinosaur lived. To find this, you must go back to the excavation site. There are plenty of clues in the sandstone rocks where you found your skeleton.

Detective work

A careful examination of the sandstone should show bits of plant material and pollen grains. These will build a picture of the plant life in the area. Sifting the sands may reveal tiny bones of small animals such as lizards or shrewlike mammals or the wings of insects. These will give us an idea of what other animals existed alongside your dinosaur. Bones of freshwater fish and shells of water snails will help prove that this was a river environment and not a seashore one.

IGUANODON HAD THREE SHORT TOES ON EACH FOOT. IT WOULD HAVE LEFT CLOVER-SHAPED FOOTPRINTS ON MUD OR DAMP SAND.

Footprints in the sands of time

The best evidence comes from traces left by the dinosaurs themselves. The study of fossil footprints has a whole science to itself, known as ichnology. Those who study fossil footprints (ichnologists) claim that their science reveals more about the living dinosaur than any number of bones can. You can see their point. In its lifetime, a single animal can leave thousands of footprints behind but only one skeleton. From the footprints, we can tell if an animal has been walking or running. If running, we can estimate the speed. We can tell if it had been traveling along a riverbank, crossing a river, or gathering around a water hole. We can tell if it moved around singly, in a pair, or as part of a herd. What we cannot tell, however, is exactly which dinosaur made which set of footprints. We may have a good guess, but there will always be an uncertainty. That is why ichnologists give fossil footprints their own scientific

A PALEONTOLOGIST EXAMINES FOSSILIZED DINOSAUR FOOTPRINTS. THE SPEED OF THE ANIMAL CAN BE CALCULATED FROM THE DISTANCE BETWEEN ITS FOOTPRINTS.

names. *Brontopodus* may be the footprints of a sauropod such as *Apatosaurus*, but we are not sure. *Tetrapodosauropus* may be the footprints of an armored dinosaur such as *Nodosaurus*, but we cannot be 100 percent certain.

Dinosaur eggs

How do you like your eggs— fried, scrambled, or boiled? Paleontologists prefer theirs to be fossilized! Dinosaur eggs, although rare, give us another glimpse into dinosaur life. Once again, there is a great deal of difficulty in matching eggs to particular dinosaurs. Sometimes we are lucky and find whole nesting sites with nests, eggs, babies, and adults, all fossilized together. Perhaps the best-known nesting site is in Montana. It is the nesting

MAIASAURA MEANS "GOOD MOTHER LIZARD." SCIENTISTS THINK THAT FEMALE *MAIASAURA* BROUGHT FOOD TO THEIR NEWLY HATCHED BABIES.

site of the hadrosaur *Maiasaura*. The nests, built of mud and twigs and about 6.5 ft (2 m) across, are spaced at regular distances from each other. In or by the nests are egg shells, baby dinosaurs, partly grown dinosaurs, and adults. *Maiasaura* laid around 30 eggs, which were roughly the same size as those of a modern ostrich. The babies may have stayed in the nest for a little while.

Oviraptor is innocent!

Some well-preserved dinosaur eggs were found in the Gobi Desert, Mongolia, in the 1920s by an expedition from the American Museum of Natural History. Among fossilized herds of the horned dinosaur *Protoceratops*, they found nests of eggs. During the late Cretaceous, the eggs had been laid in a circle in a hole scooped in sand. One even had the skeleton of a small theropod crouched over it. The theropod was named *Oviraptor*, meaning "egg thief," as it seemed to have died in the act of raiding the nest. Seventy years later, another such nest was found in Mongolia. This nest contained similar eggs, but this time a fossilized cousin of *Oviraptor*, *Citipati*, was sitting on them. So the eggs found in the 1920s were *Oviraptor* eggs all the time! The discovery of several nesting oviraptorosaurs such as *Citipati* suggests brooding was common behavior, but some scientists think these fossils represent animals

THIS IS THE SKULL OF *PROTOCERATOPS*, A FOUR-LEGGED PLANT EATER WITH A SHARP BEAK FOR CUTTING UP VEGETATION AND A LARGE, BONY NECK FRILL FOR DISPLAYING TO POTENTIAL MATES.

THIS IS A RECONSTRUCTION OF A *CITIPATI* FOSSIL THAT SHOWS A PARENT SITTING WITH THE EGGS. SCIENTISTS ARE NOT SURE IF THIS WAS THE MOTHER OR THE FATHER.

that died while laying their eggs rather than taking care of them. However, it is still plausible that these dinosaurs showed some sort of parental care once their eggs had hatched.

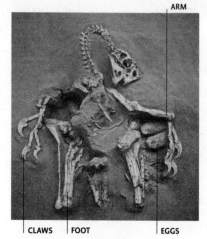

ARM

CLAWS   FOOT   EGGS

Dinosaur droppings

Coprolite—there is an impressive name. It actually means "dung stone." A coprolite is the fossil of an animal's droppings. Coprolites may sound like repulsive remains

There is one coprolite that is thought to be *Tyrannosaurus* dung, but as with footprints and eggs, it is impossible to be sure. It is 8 in (20 cm) long

to you, but paleontologists love them, and some devote themselves entirely to studying this prehistoric poop. The most common coprolites come from aquatic animals such as fish, but several dinosaur coprolites have been found. Food fragments in a coprolite can tell us about the diet of its owner, and the coprolite's shape can reveal something about the layout of the animal's digestive system.

OVIRAPTOROSAURS SUCH AS *CITIPATI* HAD A SHORT, TOOTHLESS BEAK. WHILE SOME SCIENTISTS THINK IT WAS PROBABLY A HERBIVORE, WE STILL ARE NOT SURE WHAT THIS CREATURE ATE.

and full of pieces of ornithopod dinosaur bones—just what we'd expect from guessing about *Tyrannosaurus's* hunting habits.

Stomach stones

Another guide to the diet of dinosaurs is the presence of stomach stones in the skeleton. These stones, called gastroliths, may have been swallowed by plant-eating dinosaurs to help them grind tough plant matter in the stomach. Fossils of some plant-eating theropods have been found with gastroliths in their skeleton. Because of their simple teeth and lack of chewing capabilities, it was once thought that sauropods, too, had gastroliths. This idea was based on the discovery of polished stones in the rib cages of a few specimens. Nowadays, most paleontologists agree that sauropods probably didn't have gastroliths, and the stones found among their skeletons may have been swallowed by accident.

COPROLITES MAY JUST LOOK LIKE STONES TO US, BUT TO PALEONTOLOGISTS, THEY'RE TREASURE TROVES OF DINO INFORMATION.

WEIRD WORLD

A DINOSAUR TRACKSITE IN THE STATE OF TEXAS COVERS AN AREA OF 38,600 SQ MILES (100,000 SQ KM). IT IS ONLY SEEN ON THE SURFACE IN A FEW PLACES—THE REST IS BURIED IN THE ROCKS.

OTHER LIFE AT THE TIME

By this stage, you may be thinking that dinosaurs were practically the only creatures on Earth during the Mesozoic Era. Far from it—there was a whole host of other animals around at the time. As with the dinosaurs, it's through fossils that we know of their existence.

AMMONITES WERE TENTACLED SEA CREATURES WITH SPIRAL-SHAPED SHELLS. FOSSILIZED AMMONITES ARE COMMON IN MARINE ROCKS FROM DINOSAUR TIMES.

Water beasts

We have already seen how difficult it is for a land animal such as a dinosaur to become fossilized. The best dinosaur fossils come from animals that lived near water, because their dead bodies could become buried in sediment and involved in the rock-forming processes. How much easier, then, must it be for an animal that lived in the water to become fossilized.

If you go out and look for fossils in a well-known fossil site, you'll rarely find the fossil of a dinosaur or any other large animal. What you will find are the fossils of shellfish and other animals that lived in the sea. It's not surprising really. The bodies of aquatic animals get deposited on the seabed, where sediments are continually accumulating, so their remains naturally get buried under sand, mud, or silt.

The first sea monster

The Mesozoic was truly the Age of Reptiles. Not only were dinosaurs masters of the land, but reptiles also dominated the seas and commanded the skies. The Mesozoic sea reptiles were known to scientists long before the dinosaurs were. In 1770, a fossilized jaw was unearthed in a chalk mine near Maastricht in the Netherlands. It fell into the hands of the invading French army and eventually ended up in Paris, where it was studied by Baron Georges Cuvier, the leading biologist of the day.

THE JAWS OF *MOSASAURUS* WERE LINED WITH SHARP, CONICAL TEETH. THIS REPTILE SWAM IN SHALLOW COASTAL WATERS AND WAS UP TO 33 FT (10 M) LONG.

At that time, scientists were beginning to understand that different animals had lived on Earth at different times and that many of the animals that lived in the past were now extinct. Cuvier confirmed that the fossil skull was from a type of enormous swimming lizard, which became known as *Mosasaurus*. This was one of a large family of reptiles, called

LEPIDOTES LIKELY ATE HARD-SHELLED PREY AND WAS COVERED IN THICK SCALES.

the mosasaurs, which swam by thrashing their tails back and forth. The other big reptiles of the Mesozoic were ichthyosaurs and plesiosaurs. On the coast of Dorset, in southern England, skeletons of these marine reptiles were being dug up and studied in the early 19th century.

Fishy lizards

The ichthyosaurs, or fish lizards, were originally regarded as a type of crocodile. It is easy

THE PLESIOSAUR *CRYPTOCLIDUS* HAD A SNAKELIKE NECK AND INTERLOCKING SPIKED TEETH THAT CLAMPED TIGHT AROUND FISH AND OTHER SEA CREATURES.

to see why—with their long jaws and sharp teeth, they have all the signs of a meat-eating reptile. But when more and more skeletons were discovered, it became clear that they were a totally different kind of animal.

Although they were reptiles, they were so well-adapted to their watery way of life

ICHTHYOSAURUS SWAM WITH SIDEWAYS MOVEMENTS OF ITS TAIL. LIKE OTHER MARINE REPTILES, IT HAD TO SURFACE TO FILL ITS LUNGS WITH AIR.

that they developed body shapes just like those of fish or dolphins—a streamlined body, paddles for

limbs, a fin on the tail, and a fin on the back. The fins were not originally obvious, but fossil ichthyosaurs discovered near Holzmaden in Germany were so detailed that even these soft body parts were preserved. The ichthyosaurs evolved in the Triassic, when some grew as big as whales. They flourished in the Jurassic and died out before the end of the Cretaceous.

WEIRD WORLD

WHEN A BASKING SHARK DIES, ITS HUGE JAWS FALL OFF. THE TINY-HEADED CARCASS LOOKS LIKE A ROTTING PLESIOSAUR. THIS EXPLAINS REPORTS OF DEAD PLESIOSAURS BEING FOUND ON MODERN BEACHES.

Long necks and short necks
There were two types of plesiosaurs. The long-necked types which, according to one 19th-century scientist, resembled snakes threaded through turtles, and the short-necked types, which had big heads and long jaws. Some of the short-necked ones had some of the strongest bite

forces in the animal kingdom. They evolved in the Triassic and continued until the end of the Cretaceous.

Flying reptiles

As well as reptiles powering through the oceans, there were also reptiles flapping, soaring, and swooping through the sky. The pterosaurs were a group of reptiles that, although somewhat closely related to dinosaurs, were not themselves dinosaurs. Their wings were thin flaps of skin supported by elongated fourth fingers.

Pterosaur diets depended on their size and preferred habitats. They ate a variety of prey, including fish, insects, and maybe even small dinosaurs. We have a fair number of pterosaur fossils, because many of them lived in coastal areas and fell into the sea when they died.

For the first part of the Age of Reptiles, these animals were the undisputed rulers of the skies. But in the Jurassic Period,

birds evolved from dinosaur ancestors, and by Cretaceous times, these feathery newcomers shared the skies with the pterosaurs. The first pterosaurs, the "rhamphorhynchoids," had long tails and narrow wings and included the big-beaked *Dimorphodon*. Later pterosaurs, called pterodactyloids, had short tails and broader wings. The pterodactyloids produced the biggest flying creatures that ever lived—some the size of small airplanes—during the Cretaceous Period.

Lesser lights

We have looked at the main groups of reptiles that shared the world with the dinosaurs. A vast

DIMORPHODON PROBABLY FED ON SMALL PREY. ITS LONG TAIL GAVE IT STABILITY IN THE AIR.

PTERODACTYLUS HAD A WINGSPAN OF ABOUT 20 IN (50 CM). LIKE OTHER PTERODACTYLOIDS, IT HAD A SHORT TAIL AND LONG FINGER BONES.

array of other animals lived at the time, too. The lizards and snakes evolved in the Mesozoic Era, but the most important group of vertebrates were the little furry things that scampered around the feet of the reptilian giants … the mammals. The mammals evolved in the late Triassic, at about the same time as the dinosaurs. Throughout the Age of Reptiles, they were small, insignificant, shrewlike animals. It was not until the nonbird dinosaurs died out that the mammals came into their own. But that is another story.

PTEROSAURS HAD LIGHTWEIGHT HOLLOW BONES FILLED WITH AIR

DINOSAUR HOMES

You've seen how paleontologists put together the pieces of the dinosaur jigsaw to give us a picture of life in Mesozoic times. We know what dinosaurs looked like, what they ate, how they walked, and what their eggs were like. But the picture is incomplete, as we are less certain about which dinosaurs lived in which habitat.

Where dinosaurs lived

Scientists reckon that dinosaurs colonized all the major habitats of the Mesozoic world. It's difficult to be more precise than that because many habitats were not suited to fossil formation. What do we know, for example, about dinosaurs that lived on mountaintops, where the landscape was constantly being eroded? Practically nothing. What do we know of dinosaurs that lived on windswept rocky outcrops, where

LIKE *BARYONYX*, *SUCHOMIMUS* WAS A FISH EATER THAT LIVED BESIDE RIVERS AND LAKES.

no sediments could be laid down? Zilch! What do we know of dinosaurs that lived in forests well away from rivers, where the soil was continually renewing itself with the growth and decay of plants? Not much more. On rare occasions, we find a dinosaur that was fossilized under ideal circumstances and from which we can learn a lot.

By the river

Take *Baryonyx*, for example. Almost nothing like it had ever been found before its discovery in 1983 in a clay pit in Surrey, southeastern England. It was found in river sediments by an amateur fossil collector. It was about half complete, but the bones that were present were enough to tell experts what the whole skeleton would have been like. *Baryonyx*

WEIRD WORLD
HALF AN *AMMOSAURUS* SKELETON WAS FOUND BY WORKERS BUILDING A BRIDGE IN CONNECTICUT IN THE 1880s. THE REST WAS FOUND A CENTURY LATER, WHEN A NEARBY BRIDGE WAS DEMOLISHED!

had long jaws with many sharp teeth, similar to a fish-eating crocodile. What's more, several partially digested fish scales were found in its rib cage alongside bones of a juvenile dinosaur, which suggests that *Baryonyx* had a varied diet. The Cretaceous sediments in which it was found were laid down on a boggy plain populated by dinosaurs such as *Iguanodon* and *Hypsilophodon*. So here we

WHILE SOME SCIENTISTS THINK THAT THIS *VELOCIRAPTOR* MAY HAVE BEEN HUNTING THE *PROTOCERATOPS*, OTHERS SUGGEST THAT IT MAY HAVE CHANCED UPON IT, STARTING A GRUESOME FIGHT FOR SURVIVAL.

have an instant picture of *Baryonyx*. It was a predator capable of feeding on different types of prey, allowing it to compete with other carnivores of the time.

Close relative

Baryonyx was so unusual-looking that when an almost identical animal, *Suchomimus*, was found in North Africa in 1997, scientists had absolutely no doubt that it had lived in the same kind of habitat and had the same lifestyle as *Baryonyx*. But *Suchomimus* was bigger and had a low fin down the length of its back. It was still a closely related animal that waded in rivers to hunt fish.

Secrets of the sands

Another snapshot of dinosaur life was developed in 1972. An expedition in the Gobi Desert

in Mongolia uncovered the complete skeletons of a horned *Protoceratops* and a meat-eating *Velociraptor* wrapped around one another. Tickle your cat on its tummy. What does it do? It grabs your hand and kicks away with its hind claws. That's exactly what happened here. The *Velociraptor* had seized the head-shield of the *Protoceratops*

THESE ENTWINED SKELETONS SHOW HOW A *PROTOCERATOPS* AND A *VELOCIRAPTOR* FOUGHT EACH OTHER TO THE DEATH MORE THAN 70 MILLION YEARS AGO.

and was stabbing it with the sickle-shaped killing claws on its feet. The *Protoceratops* had responded by seizing the attacker by the arm with its sharp beak. The fierce struggle was fatal for both dinosaurs. A sandstorm or a collapsing dune then buried the pair, and they were preserved until the present day.

Desert dwellers

This terrible scene tells us that early horned dinosaurs such as *Protoceratops* were prime targets for the predators of the time. But they certainly didn't give in without a fight! We also know from the numbers of remains buried in sandstorm deposits that *Protoceratops* was one of the most common animals around, dotting the landscape like

WEIRD WORLD
PROTOCERATOPS'S FRILL GREW FASTER IN COMPARISON TO THE REST OF ITS BODY. THIS PRODUCED A SKULL THAT WAS NEARLY ONE-FIFTH THE LENGTH OF THE DINOSAUR'S BODY. THE FRILL WAS PROBABLY USED TO ATTRACT POTENTIAL MATES.

sheep feeding on the sparse desert vegetation. Was *Velociraptor* a pack hunter? This is hard to say, as there is little direct evidence to support it. Fossils of its cousins suggest that they may have occasionally moved around together or fought over carcasses, but pack hunting is a complex behavior

GIGANOTOSAURUS WAS UP TO 41 FT (12.5 M) LONG AND 8.8 TONS (8 TONNES) IN WEIGHT. WE KNOW LITTLE OF ITS LIFESTYLE.

can look at the partial skeleton of *Giganotosaurus*, found in South America, and deduce that it must have been one of the biggest meat-eating dinosaurs. We can conjure up a vision of it rampaging through coniferous forests during the Cretaceous Period. We can also imagine it preying on the biggest plant eaters that ever lived— such as the giant titanosaurs, which that may have been beyond the capacities of *Velociraptor* and other theropods alike.

Forest hunter

Usually it's more difficult to say for certain where a dinosaur lived. We

lived in South America at the same time. We really do not have too much evidence for this scenario, however.

Plains runner

Then there are the skeletons of the "ostrich-mimic" dinosaurs, such as *Gallimimus*. These lightly built Cretaceous theropods are known as the ostrich mimics because of their rounded bodies and their long necks and legs. (But this comparison conveniently ignores *Gallimimus*'s long tail.) Recent studies suggest that the resemblance between ostriches and ostrich-mimic dinosaurs is superficial, but

OSTRICHES RUN FOR LONG DISTANCES OVER DRY PLAINS, TRAVELING FROM ONE FEEDING GROUND TO ANOTHER.

the idea won't go away. We see photographs of ostriches sprinting across the open plains of Africa, and it's easy to imagine herds of *Gallimimus* doing the same. Perhaps they did. But, as is often the case, hard evidence is lacking.

GALLIMIMUS MAY HAVE RUN AT UP TO 50 MPH (80 KPH)— FASTER THAN A RACEHORSE.

TRIASSIC TREK

L et us take a walk in the late Triassic Period (about 215 million years ago), after the first dinosaurs had evolved. We know enough from the paleontology and geology of the time to be able to imagine this. We had better start our walk by the sea. It is the only place that we would find comfortable or even remotely habitable.

A different world

The late Triassic world was very different from the one we know. If we wanted to go from Los Angeles, California, to Sydney, Australia, in the 21st century, we would have to fly or sail across the ocean spaces in between. But

THERE WERE NO FLOWERING PLANTS OR BROAD-LEAVED TREES IN THE TRIASSIC, BUT THERE WERE PLENTY OF HORSETAILS, FERNS, CONIFERS, AND PALMLIKE PLANTS.

in Triassic times, we could walk there, if we had enough time and energy. All the landmasses were united as a single giant supercontinent, called Pangea.

Pangea was so vast that most places in the interior were a long way from the moisture and cooling influences of the sea, so they were fiercely hot and dry. But don't worry, we won't even contemplate such an arduous journey—we'll stick to places that are less hostile.

THE TRIASSIC GLOBE. THE TETHYS SEA, A BRANCH OF THE OCEAN PANTHALASSA, WOULD LATER SPLIT PANGEA IN TWO.

By the seaside

The air is both moist and cool by the sea, but over the dusty hills, there are vast swathes of arid desert. Huge waves pound against the beach. They have had a long distance to travel

across Panthalassa—that's what we call the vast ocean that covers the rest of the Earth's surface. Great for surfing!

At your feet, the tide-line consists of shells that you have never seen before. These are mostly coiled ammonite shells whose empty chambers once held octopuslike marine animals. The tangle of seaweed looks pretty much the same as that from your own time. Among the seaweed are washed-up tree branches, mostly from conifers, ginkgos, and cycads. They must have come from a river that empties into the sea somewhere close by.

Don't touch dead things

What's that smell? In the distance lies the body of a giant ichthyosaur, like a beached whale. Long-tailed pterosaurs wheel around and squabble over the decaying flesh. Lobsterlike creatures scuttle over the corpse. The stench is strong enough to convince you not to go anywhere near that nasty mess. Leave them to

CYCADS WERE COMMON PLANTS DURING THE DINOSAUR PERIOD.

their feast. You have come here because you want to see dinosaurs, so let's go inland and do some exploring.

River safari

We walk up the bank of a river. Here, where there is moisture, there is also plenty of life. Conifers line the riverbanks, their roots in an undergrowth of ferns and mosses. Between the tree trunks, we see the desert spreading away to the horizon. There's a rustle in the undergrowth, and a little animal scampers away. A dinosaur? No, it is furry and has whiskers and little ears, like a mouse. It is one of the first mammals.

MEGAZOSTRODON WAS A SMALL
MAMMAL OF THE LATE TRIASSIC.

Our first dinosaur

Suddenly there's a
lunge and a snap!
Something snatches the
mammal from the ground and
shakes it to death. We can see
the culprit clearly—it's our
first dinosaur! The dinosaurs
and the mammals have both
recently evolved, but it's clear
from this encounter which
is the more powerful. The
dinosaur turns and runs off

between the trees,
carrying its limp
prey. We note the
dinosaur's small
body, long hind
limbs, balancing tail,
long jaws, and sharp teeth. It is
probably Herrerasaurus, one of
the earliest known dinosaurs.
It lived in parts of what is now
South America.

Giant newts

Upstream we go. The
vegetation on either side
is getting thinner as
the desert
encroaches. In the
backwaters and swamps,
we see the murky waters swirl.
What are these large shapes
moving in the murky waters?
These are giant amphibians,
like newts as big as alligators.
The time of large amphibians
is almost past, but there are
still plenty of them here. They
seem to be settling into the
mud as if they are preparing
to weather out some dry
times ahead.

HERRERASAURUS WAS A PRIMITIVE MEAT-
EATING DINOSAUR, ABOUT 10 FT (3 M) TALL.
IT HAD A SLENDER BODY, NARROW JAWS,
AND POWERFUL BACK LEGS.

A pack of mischief

Pushing forward we reach a region that will later form North America. Here the drying river has attracted a large number of *Coelophysis*. These speedy hunters have slender jaws lined with small, sharp teeth with serrated edges—perfect for snapping up lizards and other prey. They scamper and squabble as they jostle for space by the water's edge. Large numbers of *Coelophysis* are unusual, so perhaps they have come near the water in search of food in these tough times.

A hungry journey

A few *Coelophysis* peel away from the banks and head back into the forest. Some of their three-toed footprints will be preserved in the drying mud and resemble those left behind by modern birds. Here, they cross paths with a dangerous adversary—a *Postosuchus*. This massive, 19-ft (6-m) long predator is a relative of the crocodiles. It is one of a group of reptiles that flourished as much as the crocodiles in the Triassic—so much so that the dinosaurs in this time were all relatively small and rare for much of the period.

The *Coelophysis* know better than to linger, and scamper off out of harm's way.

Food at last!
It's a lucky day for this little band of *Coelophysis*, as they have stumbled upon a freshly killed *Placerias*! This mammal relative was one of the bulkiest plant eaters in the ecosystem, weighing as much as a small hippo, with two short tusks next to its mouth. The *Postosuchus* they crossed paths with earlier may have brought it down, and there's still some meat left on the body. This will certainly keep the small group fed and satisfied.

COELOPHYSIS WERE AS LONG AS A FAMILY CAR, BUT MOST OF THE LENGTH WAS TAIL AND NECK.

JURASSIC JAUNT

We are scuba diving … in the Jurassic sea! Although it is more than 150 million years ago, under the waves we see the same white sand and the same clear blue water that we see off the Bahamas in our own time. We are swimming in one of the shallow seas that is spreading over low-lying areas as Pangea begins to break up.

TETHYS SEA

PANGEA

PANTHALASSA

IN THE JURASSIC, THE SUPERCONTINENT OF PANGEA BEGAN TO SPLIT INTO FRAGMENTS THAT SLOWLY DRIFTED APART.

A warm dip in the ocean
The main difference we notice is in the shoals of swimming animals around us. Unfamiliar fish nibble on the coral growing through the sand. Bullet-shaped things that look like squid weave past us and vanish into

the distance. They must have been belemnites. Disk-shaped ammonites drift around more sedately, their big eyes looking out for prey. They are ignoring us—we're far too big for them.

Jurassic jaws
What's that dark shadow passing over us? It's an ichthyosaur on the prowl. It is a smaller, more streamlined ichthyosaur than the whalelike creature

PLESIOSAURS PROPELLED THEMSELVES GRACEFULLY THROUGH THE WATER WITH SLOW BEATS OF THEIR HUGE FLIPPERS.

we saw washed up on the Triassic beach. The ammonites draw in their tentacles and, with a squirt of ink, dart away. However, the ichthyosaur is not after them. With a flip of its tail, it cruises away in the direction of the departing belemnite shoal.

Sea serpents

Let's rise through the water and see what we can find. Hold still! There is something else here— a pair of plesiosaurs cruising just below the surface. Don't panic! Control your

ABOUT 23 FT (7 M) LONG, A PLIOSAUR WAS A FIERCE OCEAN HUNTER OF FISH AND SMALL SEA REPTILES IN THE LATE JURASSIC.

breathing or you won't be able to see through the bubbles. And try not to be noticed. It's okay, the plesiosaurs are more interested in fish. They move slowly, using their four long flippers to propel themselves through the water. Their heads, on their long necks, are turning this way and that, their long teeth ready to snap at any fish that comes within range.

A SMALL TAIL FIN HELPED PLESIOSAURS IN STEERING THROUGH THE WATER.

FLEXIBLE LONG NECK

PADDLELIKE FLIPPERS

Reptiles of the sky

We break the surface. Luckily we are not far from the shore. The landscape seems to be low-lying and thickly-vegetated. There are dark shapes above. Are they birds? But their big heads and leathery wings show them to be pterosaurs. We can spot both long-tailed and short-tailed types.

Beachcombers

On the beach on this island, one of many that make up what is now Europe, we see a little chicken-sized dinosaur scampering along the sand, pursuing a lizard. It must be *Compsognathus*, because that's one of the smallest Jurassic dinosaurs we know of. The lizard weaves and dodges up the beach, disappearing beneath the arching fronds of the ferny

undergrowth. The *Compsognathus* gives chase. Suddenly a dreadful commotion erupts from the foliage. A feathered form leaps disturbed from the undergrowth and flaps clumsily toward the low-hanging branches of a conifer tree. It is *Archaeopteryx*, an early bird. It settles on a branch on all fours—it has claws on its "hands," as well as its feet—because it is not very good at perching. The flustered *Archaeopteryx* keeps a watchful eye at the many reptiles in the undergrowth. So there are birds here after all!

AGILE AND QUICK-FOOTED, *COMPSOGNATHUS* ATE CREATURES SUCH AS SNAILS, LIZARDS, INSECTS, AND FROGS.

Green landscape

Ready to go into the forest? It could be dangerous. The vegetation, as in the Triassic forests of what is now North America, consists of conifer and ginkgo trees and cycads, with an undergrowth of horsetails and ferns. However, there seems to be so much more of it. The air is not as dry as it was during the Triassic, and the land is

ARCHAEOPTERYX WAS A PRIMITIVE BIRD WITH TEETH, A BONY TAIL, WEAK FLAPPING MUSCLES, AND CLAWS ON ITS WINGS.

much greener. The oceans that are creeping in along the deep valleys formed by the splitting of Pangea, and the shallow seas that are

ARCHAEOPTERYX WAS PROBABLY CAPABLE OF SHORT BURSTS OF FLIGHT

spreading over the land, are producing wetter climates. In fact, it is beginning to rain.

The forest browsers
Pushing onward through the wet forest, knee-high in sodden ferns and with dripping boughs splashing cold drops on our heads, we suddenly find ourselves in an open clearing. We are on a floodplain. A huge herd of beasts stands at one end of the clearing, their long necks reaching around like vacuum-cleaner hoses to munch the undergrowth as they go. The clearing is caused by them ripping up the vegetation. They are obviously

sauropods of some kind, probably *Barosaurus* or one of the other long, low types.

There are about a dozen *Barosaurus* in the herd. Now and again, they reach up to scrape needles from one of the conifer trees. Their weak bites mean they prefer eating softer plants. They have heard us. One utters a loud steam-whistle hiss. They all look up, raising their little heads on their long necks. They then troop off across a shallow, rain-dappled river. The soil of the riverbank is trampled and churned underfoot. In millions of years' time, the rocks formed here will not have the crisp, well-defined layers that geologists would normally expect to find in rocks formed from river sediments. Instead, they will be all stirred up and mixed by the messy *Barosaurus* footprints—"bioturbation" is the fancy name that geologists give to this action.

The rich vegetation supports many hungry herbivores, and several huge plant eaters march through the landscape looking to fill their stomach. However, where there are plant eaters, there are meat eaters, too, looking for any opportunity for an easy meal. We don't want to draw too much attention to ourselves, so we'd better tread carefully and try not to make too much noise.

Trouble!
Keeping an eye open for theropods of all shapes and sizes, we continue our exploration of

---

DESERTS BEGAN TO DISAPPEAR DURING THE JURASSIC, BUT THE CLIMATE WAS STILL WARMER THAN IT IS TODAY.

the forest. But, just our luck, it is one of the big ones that spots us. An *Allosaurus* emerges from behind a tree and notices us the very moment we notice it. Before long, its brain registers that we are potential food. With a low hiss, it opens its wicked mouth and charges. Run! We take to our heels, dodging around tree trunks to try to shake off our bloodthirsty pursuer. We start to panic as we realize that this large animal is gaining on us!

A welcome diversion

Suddenly, we find ourselves in open country. The forested areas are separated by large open stretches. And there in front of us, lazily swinging its tail and casting shadows with the broad, diamond-shaped plates on its back, stands a *Stegosaurus*. The plated plant eater seems to prefer the clearings to the confined forests. Out in the open, its plates will not become entangled in branches.

DILOPHOSAURUS, OF THE EARLY JURASSIC, WAS ONE OF THE FIRST LARGE THEROPODS. THE CREST ON ITS HEAD WAS PROBABLY USED TO ATTRACT MATES.

ALLOSAURUS WAS
ABOUT 25 FT (9 M)
LONG AND HAD A
STRONG SKULL FILLED
WITH SERRATED TEETH.

The *Allosaurus* plunges
out of the greenery
behind us and halts
abruptly, distracted by
the plated dinosaur.
We do not expect the
Stegosaurus to run away.

Look at those
hind legs. The thigh
is longer than the shin.
This is a sign of a
slow-moving animal.
The *Stegosaurus* will
stand its ground.
We expect a fight,
but we are
disappointed.
The *Allosaurus*
turns and stalks

back into the greenery. It's more interested in picking off a young or sickly *Barosaurus* from the herd than staying here and tussling with the *Stegosaurus*.

That was a lucky escape for us. As the Sun goes down over the Jurassic landscape, silhouetting a herd of *Brachiosaurus* against the fading light, we realize that this is no place for humans.

ALLOSAURUS WOULD SELDOM ATTACK AN ADULT *BRACHIOSAURUS* WEIGHING ABOUT 55 TONS (50 TONNES), BUT THE SAUROPOD'S YOUNG WERE SOMETIMES A TARGET.

CRETACEOUS CROSSING

Now we are white-water rafting in the highlands of Late Cretaceous North America, about 70 million years ago. We can call places by modern names, because Pangea has broken up into the individual continents, which are slowly drifting into their familiar positions.

Rafting in the Rockies

The current carries us down the mountain river at breakneck speed. These mountains are the young Rockies, thrust up as the continent of North America pushes westward against the floor of the Pacific

FLOWERING PLANTS BEGAN TO TAKE OVER FROM FERNS, HORSETAILS, AND CYCADS. THERE WERE MODERN-LOOKING CONIFERS AND BROAD-LEAVED TREES.

Ocean, wrinkling up the rocks along the edge as it goes. The rocks are sediments laid down in Triassic and Jurassic times—we can see fossils of *Coelophysis* footprints and ichthyosaur bones in the crags that rise around us. Up here in the windy heights, there are few animals to be seen. The dark shapes of giant pterosaurs swoop around the cloudy peaks in the distance. These are pterodactyloids, the short-tailed type of pterosaur. (The long-tailed types, the "rhamphorhynchoids", have all died out by now.) But the flying things in the mountain bushes nearby are all birds.

AS THE CONTINENTS DRIFTED APART, THE WORLD STARTED TO TAKE ON A MORE FAMILIAR SHAPE TO MODERN EYES.

PACHYCEPHALOSAURUS WAS A
DOME-HEADED DINOSAUR. RIVAL
MALES MAY HAVE SETTLED
DISPUTES OVER FEMALES
OR TERRITORY BY BUTTING
ONE ANOTHER WITH
THEIR DOMED SKULLS.

shelf, two
dome-headed
pachycephalosaurs
drink from the water.
They are startled
to see us and quickly
disappear into
the forest.
Where they
vanished, a broad,
armored back can be
seen rising above the ferns.

AN ANKYLOSAUR'S WEAK SPOT
WAS ITS SOFT, UNPROTECTED BELLY

Mountain vegetation
The torrent carries us onward
through the gorges, over rapids,
and down toward the foothills.
The current eases as we drift
along. Conifers with a ferny
undergrowth line the banks.

Beasts ahoy!
We round a corner and come
across our first big animals.
On the inside of the river
bend, where some flat rocks
form a partly submerged

THE LARGE SHOULDER SPIKES
OF EDMONTONIA WERE
COVERED IN TOUGH
KERATIN AND
WERE POSSIBLY
USED IN
DISPLAY.

An ankylosaur of some kind pushes through the undergrowth, its head down as it feeds from the low-growing plants. As we pass by, we see that it is one of the side-spiked ankylosaurs, like *Edmontonia*. However, it is difficult to see the exact arrangement of armor, so we cannot be sure of its identity.

Ankylosaur armor is often found upside down, as if the dead body had floated downstream and turned over as it decayed. The most common fossils from pachycephalosaurs, however, are of the solid skulls, as these are the bones that will most likely be fossilized compared to the smaller, more delicate bones of the rest of the body. This suggests that they lived in upland areas.

Modern plants

Now the vegetation begins to change. As we float farther downstream, the plant life becomes more colorful. The undergrowth consists of little yellow flowers that resemble buttercups. Bushes with big blooms, such as magnolias, line the banks. The primitive conifers of the higher slopes are now replaced by trees that look like willows and

THE MAGNOLIA FAMILY IS A SURVIVOR FROM CRETACEOUS TIMES, WHEN FLOWERING SPECIES BECAME THE DOMINANT PLANT GROUP.

oaks. We could almost be looking at the vegetation of our own time, but something seems to be missing and we cannot tell what that is.

Plains migrants

Before long, the river leaves the forests of the hills and meanders over a lowland plain. *Pachyrhinosaurus* and other horned dinosaurs of the ceratopsian group live here. We spy herds of them following us down the stream. This does not surprise us—in our own time, we have seen pictures of herds of plant-eating animals, such as buffalo or wildebeest, traveling across the floodplains. Here, the situation must be the same. There is safety in numbers—after all, this is a land of tyrannosaurs.

A watery grave

We notice well-trodden banks where the ceratopsian herds have been scrambling through

PACHYRHINOSAURUS PROBABLY MOVED IN HERDS—MANY OF THEIR BONES HAVE BEEN RECOVERED TOGETHER IN HUGE MASS GRAVES. THESE HERDS MAY HAVE RUN INTO HERDS OF OTHER PLANT-EATERS SUCH AS *EDMONTOSAURUS*.

mud to cross the river. There must be many disasters as herds are caught and washed away in flash floods. You can just imagine the panic and struggle as terrified animals trample and crush one another, and the crocodiles wait patiently for the losers.

Hadrosaurs, the other major plant-eating group that dominated the Late Cretaceous Period, mingle around the river's edge. With their unique and complex teeth, they are able to chew through tough food, and they often form social groups like the *Pachyrhinosaurus*.

End of an era

The Late Cretaceous saw some of the most famous dinosaurs briefly take to the throne. The *Pachyrhinosaurus* we saw earlier had already disappeared, but many horned cousins evolved in their place, as did new types of hadrosaurs. With our backpacks on and our walking boots laced up, we set off to explore the last few days of the dinosaurs. As we trudge across the forests and plains that cover the area, we see the last of the sauropods.

Dangerous country

Walking in the warm sunlight, a group of *Edmontosaurus*—a type of hadrosaur with a broad,

curved beak—trot past, making all sorts of racket. They sound like alarm calls; something must have spooked them.

It is not long before we see what it was that frightened the herd of *Edmontosaurus*. A big *Tyrannosaurus* is crouched over the body of a freshly killed hadrosaur, tearing it apart. As we watch, it is joined by another *Tyrannosaurus*. A rival or a mate?

Close combat

The meat eaters emit low, raspy hisses as they clash until the weaker predator gets the message. After a few of these half-hearted

SALTASAURUS, OF THE LATE CRETACEOUS, WAS RELATIVELY SMALL FOR A SAUROPOD. IT HAD BONY PLATES AND NODULES SET INTO THE SKIN OF ITS BACK.

71

hisses, it turns and stalks away through the forest. Would it be wise to follow this beast to see where it goes? Maybe not, but let's take the risk. We lose sight of it briefly, but suddenly there

is an eruption of hisses. It seems to have gotten into a fight.

Teeth against horns
And what a fight it is! A *Triceratops*, one of the biggest and strongest of the ceratopsians, has been startled by the defeated *Tyrannosaurus* and is not impressed by its presence ... a big mistake! The two are now circling

WITH SHARP TEETH POWERED BY STRONG JAWS, THIS *TYRANNOSAURUS* WOULD NOT TAKE LONG TO OVERPOWER THE *TRICERATOPS*.

one another, trying to intimidate their opponent. We look for a thick clump of grass to hide behind, but we cannot see one. Now we realize what is missing from Cretaceous vegetation. Despite the modern look to the plants, there is no grass at all. Grasses had only recently evolved, and they were not as widespread as they are today. Suddenly, the landscape seems alien and threatening. We should leave. A scampering in the undergrowth shows where tiny mammals of this time—little different from the one we saw in the Triassic—still run and hide from the great reptiles. So the environment is not as familiar as we first thought—it is still the domain of the dinosaurs. Oh, and the fight? Well, it seems we have a clear victor.

AND THEN THERE WERE NONE!

The dinosaurs were one of the most successful animals on Earth for 180 million years. (Humans have only been around for a mere 300,000 years.) However, the nonbird dinosaurs disappeared about 66 million years ago. What caused this? Scientists have been piecing together what may have happened to these spectacular animals.

End-Cretaceous extinction

Late Cretaceous rocks are full of fossils of nonbird dinosaurs. However, the rocks of the early Paleogene Period (the period after the Cretaceous) have none. There is a sharp boundary between the two. It was not only the nonbird dinosaurs that died out by the end of the Cretaceous, but a host of other things perished as well. Gone were the flying pterosaurs, as well as the swimming mosasaurs and plesiosaurs. The ammonites and belemnites also died out, as did many kinds of fish.

The birds also suffered considerable losses, with several groups becoming extinct. Only a handful of ground-dwelling, seed-eating forms survived the event and took over from the pterosaurs as the masters of the skies.

Even the mammals weren't spared, but some were able to tough it out in burrows until the worst of it had passed. They went on to replace the dinosaurs as the dominant land animals.

A WELL-PRESERVED BELEMNITE FOSSIL. BELEMNITES WERE ONE OF THE MANY GROUPS OF INVERTEBRATE (ANIMAL WITHOUT A BACKBONE) THAT DIED OUT AT THE END OF THE CRETACEOUS.

Asteroid impact

The extinction of the nonbird dinosaurs 66 million years ago was a sudden event. Imagine that you are watching the skies. In an instant, everything is engulfed in a dazzling light as an asteroid—a large rock from space—blasts through the atmosphere and explodes just behind the horizon. A few seconds later, the shock wave pounds you to pieces where you stand. That is sudden!

If you are a few hundred miles away, the shock wave will take several minutes to reach you. If you are not killed instantly, you will be hammered by flying stones and branches. Red-hot fragments will rain down from the sky. The impact of the asteroid casts up an

WHAM! SHOCK WAVES RACE ACROSS THE GLOBE AS A GIANT ASTEROID CRASHES INTO EARTH.

HUGE OCEAN WAVES MAY HAVE POUNDED THE LOW-LYING LANDS AFTER THE ASTEROID IMPACT, SWEEPING AWAY ALL LIFE.

enormous ocean wave that sweeps inland, destroying everything in its path.

Even on the other side of the world, you will not be safe. You may well survive the initial

shock wave, feeling it like a distant earthquake, but dust, smoke, and steam thrown up into the atmosphere will prevent much of the Sun's light and heat from reaching Earth's surface. Over the next few months, all the plants will die. You will have no food. It will become cold. This nightmare scenario is not just guesswork—there is evidence to support the idea that an asteroid may have changed the course of life on Earth.

Evidence of the impact
In rocks that were laid down at the end of the Cretaceous Period, there are traces of the

RINGS OF MOUNTAINS WOULD HAVE MARKED THE IMPACT SITE FOR SEVERAL MILLION YEARS AFTERWARD.

element iridium. This element is not often found on Earth but is common in asteroids. Scientists have also discovered a vast asteroid impact buried beneath the Yucatán Peninsula, Mexico, which dates from about the right time. What's more, beds of debris apparently laid down by giant waves have been found in rocks from the southern US. All of this suggests that an asteroid the size of a small city struck Earth about 66 million years ago.

Lots of lava

For several hundred thousand years before the asteroid hit Earth, huge volcanic eruptions were belching out gases in what is now modern-day India. Some scientists have suggested that

VAST OUTPOURINGS OF LAVA ARE USUALLY ACCOMPANIED BY GAS AND STEAM CLOUDS THAT CAN ALTER THE CLIMATE.

the rise in global temperatures from these gases may have contributed to the end-

EVEN THE BEST FOSSILIZED DINOSAUR EXAMPLES LIKE THIS *EDMONTOSAURUS* FOSSIL TELL US NOTHING ABOUT WHAT WIPED THEM OUT.

Cretaceous extinction. Recent research, however, suggests that these climate changes were over long before the asteroid crashed into Earth. This means that the massive space rock may have been the only cause of the mass extinction event.

A regular event

Whatever happened to wipe out the nonbird dinosaurs and the other animals of the time, it was not so unusual. Mass extinctions of this scale have happened about five times in Earth's history. Think of all the animals that have become extinct in the last few hundred years—the dodo, the passenger pigeon, and the Tasmanian wolf, to name just a few.

Indeed, humans are playing a role in the extinction of many of today's life forms. The climate is getting warmer, forests are being cut down, and oceans are becoming more acidic as a result of human activity. If this goes unchecked there may be another mass extinction on its way.

WEIRD WORLD

IF THE NONBIRD DINOSAURS HAD NOT BECOME EXTINCT, WE WOULD NOT BE HERE NOW. IT WAS THEIR DISAPPEARANCE THAT ALLOWED THE MAMMALS TO BECOME THE DOMINANT ANIMALS ON EARTH.

DRAMATIC CHANGES IN CLIMATE, SUCH AS EARTH BECOMING HOTTER AND DRIER, MAY HAVE ALSO CONTRIBUTED TOWARD THE END-CRETACEOUS EXTINCTION.

THE DINOSAUR'S CHANGING FACE

The first dinosaur pictures and models looked very different from the ones we see today. We may be tempted to laugh at these early efforts, but they weren't bad considering that dinosaur pioneers had just a few bones and teeth to go on. The rest had to be clever guesswork.

The first restoration

If somebody gave you, say, an eye and a toenail and asked you to draw the animal that they came from, you could draw a very strange beast indeed, or you could draw something that you knew. This is pretty much how the first discoverers of dinosaur remains had to work.

In the 1820s, Dr. Gideon Mantell and his wife Mary discovered fossilized bones and teeth in the Cretaceous rocks of Sussex, in southern England. Mantell was a country doctor who studied fossils as a hobby. He knew that these were reptile bones, and the teeth were like giant versions of those found in the modern plant-eating iguana lizard. That was all he knew. It is hardly surprising then that his restoration looked like a giant iguana. And that is why he named the animal *Iguanodon*, meaning "iguana-toothed."

A name for the giant reptiles

Sir Richard Owen, the most famous British naturalist of his day, invented the name "dinosaur" in 1842. At that time, there had been only three dinosaurs found: the ornithopod *Iguanodon*,

THE IGUANA LIZARD WAS LIKENED TO A DINOSAUR BY EARLY PALEONTOLOGISTS.

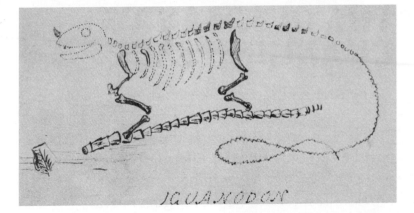

MANTELL'S FIRST SKETCH OF *IGUANODON* SHOWS A FOUR-FOOTED LIZARD.

the theropod *Megalosaurus*, and the ankylosaur *Hylaeosaurus*. (We still do not know a lot about that last one.) Soon it became like it is today— everyone was fascinated by dinosaurs and wanted to know more. When the Crystal Palace park was opened in London, England, in 1854, parts of the grounds were turned into the first dinosaur theme park. Concrete statues of all the dinosaurs known were set up, along with statues of the sea reptiles and pterosaurs. They are still there today—totally inaccurate, but reflecting the state of knowledge at the time.

THE CRYSTAL PALACE STATUES REFLECT WONDERFULLY THE 19TH-CENTURY KNOWLEDGE OF DINOSAURS.

IF WE ONLY HAD THE SKULL OF A RABBIT TO GO ON, WE WOULDN'T BE ABLE TO TELL THAT WHEN IT WAS ALIVE IT HAD CHUBBY CHEEKS, LONG EARS, AND FUR.

New discoveries

The first American dinosaur skeleton was found in the 1850s. It was a partial skeleton of a *Hadrosaurus* found in New Jersey and described by Joseph Leidy, a professor of anatomy. The skeleton showed an animal whose hind legs were longer than its front ones, suggesting that it walked on two legs.

Then came an even better discovery. More than 30 *Iguanodon* skeletons were found in a Belgian mine in 1878, and most of those were complete and still joined together. Now people were getting a better idea of what dinosaurs were like.

Images based on evidence

A restoration is only as good as the evidence available. Imagine you had been given a pile of, let's say, rabbit skeletons, and most of those were still joined together.

If you had never seen a

THIS MODERN RECONSTRUCTION OF *MANTELLISAURUS*, A CLOSE COUSIN OF *IGUANODON*, SHOWS AN ANIMAL WITH A HORIZONTAL BACKBONE. IT PROBABLY SPENT MOST OF ITS TIME ON ALL FOURS.

rabbit and you were asked to draw a restoration of one based only on those skeletons, what would the result be? You probably would not give it the rounded, furry cheeks that hide the big, gnawing teeth. You certainly would not know that it was supposed to have long ears. And what about the white cottontail? The picture you drew would be closer to a real rabbit than one drawn from just an eye and a toenail, but it would still not be accurate. Based

COMPLETE DINOSAUR SKELETONS ARE VERY RARE

THIS EARLY RECONSTRUCTION OF *IGUANODON* SHOWED AN UPRIGHT ANIMAL SITTING ON ITS TAIL LIKE A KANGAROO.

on the Belgian skeletons and the finds from America, ornithopods such as *Iguanodon* and *Hadrosaurus* were shown as upright animals. And that is how things stayed for nearly 100 years.

Iguanodon today

By the mid-20th century, scientists had learned more about how animals are built and the way that they interact with their environment. They could also apply engineering principles to dinosaur skeletons to show how they moved. Large ornithopods were now restored as four-footed animals that held their tails clear of the ground. They only rose on their hind legs now and again. Nowadays, we can build what we are sure is a pretty accurate restoration of an *Iguanodon*. Look at the picture below. Yes, you've figured it out—we've been using restorations throughout the book. We are luckier than Dr. Mantell, nearly 200 years ago. We not only have a lot more knowledge about the lives and habits of animals of the past, but we can also use science, computer wizardry, and imagination to reconstruct the amazing world of the dinosaurs.

THIS RESTORATION OF *IGUANODON* MAY CHANGE AS NEW DISCOVERIES ARE MADE.

WEIRD WORLD

TO CELEBRATE THE COMPLETION OF THE CRYSTAL PALACE DINOSAURS, A SPECIAL NEW YEAR'S EVE DINNER WAS HELD— INSIDE THE HOLLOW CONCRETE MODEL OF AN *IGUANODON*!

REFERENCE SECTION

Whether you've finished reading *Dinosaurs* or are turning to this section first, you'll find the information on the next eight pages really useful. Here are all the facts and figures, background details, meanings of dinosaur names, and unfamiliar words that you might need. There's also a list of website addresses—so whether you want to surf the net or search out facts, these pages should turn you from an enthusiast into an expert.

DINOSAURS IN THIS BOOK

NAME OF DINOSAUR	MEANING OF NAME	WHEN IT LIVED (period/millions of years ago)	
Herrerasaurus	Herrera's lizard	Triassic	231 mya
Hypsilophodon	High-ridged tooth	Cretaceous	125 mya
Ankylosaurs			
Ankylosaurus	Fused lizard	Cretaceous	66 mya
Borealopelta	Northern shield	Cretaceous	110 mya
Edmontonia	From Edmonton	Cretaceous	73 mya
Euoplocephalus	Well-shielded head	Cretaceous	75 mya
Hylaeosaurus	Forest lizard	Cretaceous	138 mya
Nodosaurus	Knobbed lizard	Cretaceous	100 mya
Ceratopsians			
Pachyrhinosaurus	Thick-nosed lizard	Cretaceous	70 mya
Protoceratops	First horned face	Cretaceous	75 mya
Psittacosaurus	Parrot lizard	Cretaceous	120 mya
Styracosaurus	Spear-spike lizard	Cretaceous	75 mya
Triceratops	Three-horned face	Cretaceous	66 mya
Ornithopods			
Brachylophosaurus	Short-crested lizard	Cretaceous	78 mya
Corythosaurus	Helmet lizard	Cretaceous	74 mya
Edmontosaurus	Lizard of Edmonton	Cretaceous	66 mya
Hadrosaurus	Sturdy lizard	Cretaceous	79 mya
Iguanodon	Iguana tooth	Cretaceous	125 mya
Maiasaura	Good mother lizard	Cretaceous	75 mya
Mantellisaurus	Mantell's lizard	Cretaceous	125–110 mya
Pachycephalosaurs			
Pachycephalosaurus	Thick-headed lizard	Cretaceous	66 mya
Stegoceras	Roof horn	Jurassic	76 mya
"Prosauropods"			
Ammosaurus	Sand lizard	Jurassic	197 mya

TIMELINE OF PERIODS AND ERAS

298 MILLION YEARS AGO	252 MILLION YEARS AGO	201 MILLION YEARS AGO
Permian Period	Triassic Period	Jurassic Period
Paleozoic Era	Mesozoic Era	

Sauropods

Apatosaurus	Deceptive lizard	Jurassic	152 mya
Argentinosaurus	Lizard of Argentina	Cretaceous	93 mya
Barosaurus	Heavy lizard	Jurassic	150 mya
Brachiosaurus	Arm lizard	Jurassic	152 mya
Diplodocus	Double beam	Jurassic	152 mya
Saltasaurus	Salta lizard	Cretaceous	80 mya
Sauroposeidon	Poseidon's lizard	Cretaceous	115 mya

Stegosaurs

Stegosaurus	Roofed lizard	Jurassic	152 mya

Theropods

Albertosaurus	Lizard of Alberta	Cretaceous	70 mya
Allosaurus	Strange lizard	Jurassic	152 mya
Archaeopteryx	Ancient wing	Jurassic	150 mya
Bambiraptor	Baby robber	Cretaceous	72 mya
Baryonyx	Heavy claw	Cretaceous	125 mya
Citipati	Funeral pyre lord	Cretaceous	75 mya
Coelophysis	Hollow form	Triassic	215 mya
Compsognathus	Dainty jaw	Jurassic	150 mya
Deinonychus	Terrible claw	Cretaceous	113 mya
Dilophosaurus	Double-crested lizard	Triassic	193 mya
Eoraptor	Dawn robber	Triassic	231 mya
Gallimimus	Chicken mimic	Cretaceous	70 mya
Giganotosaurus	Giant southern lizard	Cretaceous	98 mya
Megalosaurus	Big lizard	Jurassic	165 mya
Microraptor	Small robber	Cretaceous	125 mya
Ornitholestes	Bird stealer	Jurassic	154 mya
Ornithomimus	Bird mimic	Cretaceous	70 mya
Oviraptor	Egg robber	Cretaceous	80 mya
Spinosaurus	Spined lizard	Cretaceous	110 mya
Suchomimus	Crocodile mimic	Cretaceous	112 mya
Tyrannosaurus	Tyrant lizard	Cretaceous	66 mya
Utahraptor	Utah robber	Cretaceous	125 mya
Velociraptor	Fast robber	Cretaceous	75 mya

145 MILLION YEARS AGO		66 MILLION YEARS AGO	NOW
Cretaceous Period		Tertiary & Quaternary Periods	
Mesozoic Era		Cenozoic Era	

MILESTONES OF DISCOVERY

1822 James Parkinson, a doctor, gives the unofficial name *Megalosaurus* to a jawbone found in Oxfordshire, England.

1824 Dean William Buckland, a clergyman, publishes a scientific description of *Megalosaurus*—the first serious study of a dinosaur.

1825 Dr. Gideon Mantell publishes a description of *Iguanodon*.

1837 Paleontologist Hermann von Meyer publishes a description of *Plateosaurus*.

1842 Naturalist Sir Richard Owen invents the name "Dinosauria," later shortened to dinosaur.

1854 Life-sized dinosaur statues unveiled at Crystal Palace in London.

1858 Anatomist Joseph Leidy publishes a description of *Hadrosaurus*, the first North American discovery.

1859 The publication of Charles Darwin's book *The Origin of Species* puts the dinosaurs' development into an evolutionary context.

1860 First discovery of the early bird *Archaeopteryx* in Germany.

1870s–1890s In the US, fossil hunters Othniel Marsh and Edward Cope compete with one another for the best fossil discoveries. This bitter dispute becomes known as the "bone wars." More than 130 new dinosaurs are discovered during this period.

1878 Over 30 *Iguanodon* skeletons are found in Belgium, giving a good idea of dinosaur anatomy.

1887 Paleontologist Henry Seeley sets up the lizard-hip/bird-hip classification system.

1909–1913 German expeditions unearth the first dinosaur skeletons in Africa.

1922 American expeditions in the Gobi Desert led by Roy Chapman Andrews find the first undisputed dinosaur eggs in the Gobi Desert.

1938 Serious study of dinosaur footprints begins with R. T. Bird's discovery of fossil tracks in Texas.

1944 Allied bombing destroys valuable African specimens in Berlin, Germany, and also a dinosaur theme park, Hagenbeck's, in Hamburg.

1960s John Ostrom revolutionizes dino studies by suggesting they were warm-blooded and gave rise to birds.

1974 Robert Bakker and Peter Galton group all dinosaurs as descendents from a common ancestor.

1980 Luis and Walter Alvarez suggest that dinosaur extinction was due to an asteroid impact.

1986 The first dinosaur discovery, of an ankylosaur, in Antarctica.

1990s American expeditions to Madagascar find many important dinosaur remains.

1996 The first of many feathered dinosaurs is found in China.

2010 Pigments are discovered in the feathers of a small theropod, revealing its colors.

2010 *Asilisaurus* is discovered, revealing new information about the dinosaur's closest fossil cousins.

2017 Matthew Barron and colleagues propose a radically different dinosaur family tree.

2018 Part of a dinosaur tail is found preserved in amber.

TRADITIONAL FAMILY TREE

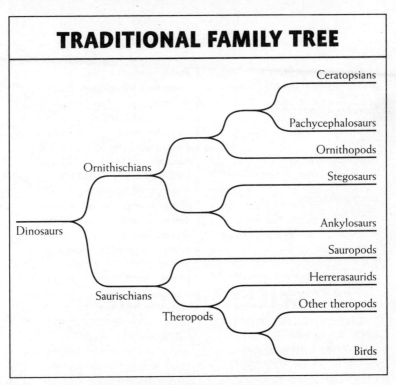

DINOSAUR WEBSITES

https://iknowdino.com
Hear podcasts about dinosaurs, including interviews with paleontologists.
http://www.bbc.co.uk/earth/tags/dinosaur
Read articles and see videos about dinosaurs.
https://www.nhm.ac.uk/discover/dino-directory.html
Discover facts, images, and other information about dinosaurs from A to Z.
https://www.amnh.org/dinosaurs
The American Museum of Natural History website's dinosaur section has articles, videos, and information about new dinosaur exhibits at the museum.
https://www.dkfindout.com/uk/dinosaurs-and-prehistoric-life/dinosaurs/
Search for your favorite dinosaur and find out more about their life, diet, and body structure.
https://blog.everythingdinosaur.co.uk/
Read up on new discoveries being made across the world in dinosaur studies.

DINO RECORDS

Longest dinosaur known
Argentinosaurus, about 131 ft (40 m).

Heaviest dinosaur known
Argentinosaurus, about 90 tons
(82 tonnes).

Biggest predator
Tyrannosaurus, about 9.9 tons (9 tonnes).

Longest predator
Spinosaurus, about 49 ft (15 m).

Smallest nonbird dinosaur known
Compsognathus, about 40 in (1 m) long.

Fastest runners
A group of theropods called
ornithomimids, possibly reached
speeds of 31 mph (50 kph).

First dinosaur in space
Coelophysis—a fossil was taken up
in the Space Shuttle in 1998.

[These figures only refer to the
dinosaurs we know, and we think
that we know only about one-third
of the dinosaurs that existed.]

SCIENTIFIC STUDIES

The two main sciences involved in the study of dinosaurs are geology (the study of the Earth) and biology (the study of life). Within these sciences are many other studies …

Paleontology The study of ancient life. Under this banner come various studies, such as invertebrate paleontology and vertebrate paleontology, and also some of the following terms.

Biogeography The study of what animals and plants are found in different places and why they occur there.

Ichnology The study of footprints and other trace fossils.

Paleobotany The study of ancient plant life.

Paleozoology The study of ancient animal life.

Paleogeography The study of the ancient landforms—the positions of the continents, the climates, and the environmental conditions at different periods of geological time.

Sedimentology The study of the formation of sediments and sedimentary rocks in which fossils are found.

Stratigraphy The study of the layers of sedimentary rocks, the sequence in which they were laid down, and the conditions under which they formed.

Systematics The study of the diversity of organisms and their relationships to one another.

Taphonomy The study of what happens to dead organisms before they become fossilized.

Taxonomy The practice of naming different organisms on the basis of their relationships.

DINOSAUR GLOSSARY

Ammonite
A Mesozoic marine animal, like an octopus with a coiled shell.

Amphibian
A type of small, cold-blooded vertebrate that starts life in water as a tadpole and turns into an air-breathing adult, such as a frog, that can live on land.

Ankylosaur
An armored, bird-hipped dinosaur.

Asteroid
A chunk of rock that orbits the Sun. Asteroids vary greatly in size.

Belemnite
An extinct, squidlike invertebrate with an internal shell.

Ceratopsian
A horned, bird-hipped dinosaur.

Conifer
A seed-bearing tree that reproduces by means of cones.

Coprolite
A fossilized animal dropping.

Cretaceous
The period of time lasting from 145 to 66 million years ago. The last of the three periods in the Mesozoic Era.

Cycad
A primitive seed-bearing plant. Cycads look like palm trees but are more closely related to conifers.

Diagenesis
The process by which sediments turn into sedimentary rock.

Dromeosaurid
A group of small to midsized theropods famous for their curved "killer claws" on their feet.

Environment
The surroundings of an animal or plant—including the climate, the landscape, the altitude, the other animals, and the plants living there.

Erosion
The natural process whereby exposed rocks are broken down and worn away.

Flash flood
A sudden flood that sweeps down a river following heavy rain upstream.

Fossil
The remains of a once-living thing preserved in rock.

Gastrolith
A stone swallowed by an animal to help in its digestion.

Ginkgo
A type of tree with fan-shaped leaves.

Glass fiber
A tough building material consisting of hairs of glass embedded in resin.

Horsetail
A primitive plant related to ferns that consists of a vertical stem with regular whorls of leaves.

Ichnology
The study of footprints.

Ichthyosaur
A fish-shaped marine reptile common in the Mesozoic Era.

Iguana
A modern-day plant-eating lizard from South and Central America.

Intestines
Tubes in the body through which food passes and which absorb nutrients.

Invertebrate
An animal without a backbone.

Jurassic Period
The second period of the Mesozoic Era. The Jurassic lasted from 201 to 145 million years ago.

Laboratory
A place where scientific work is done.

Mace
A clublike ancient weapon that consisted of a heavy head at the end of a rigid shaft.

Mammal
A type of hairy, warm-blooded, vertebrate animal whose females produce milk and suckle their young. Humans are mammals.

Mass extinction
An event during which many different types of animals and plants die out.

Mesozoic Era
The era of history stretching from 252 to 66 million years ago. It includes the Triassic, Jurassic, and Cretaceous Periods. The era preceding the Mesozoic was the Paleozoic, when life began to move from the sea to the land. The era following the Mesozoic was the Cenozoic, which includes the Age of Mammals and brings us up to the present day.

Migrate
To travel from one area to another, usually in response to changing living conditions such as climate or the availability of food.

Mineral
An inorganic substance that is formed naturally by geological processes. Rocks are accumulations of minerals.

Mosasaur
A sea-living reptile from the Cretaceous Period closely related to modern monitor lizards.

Muscle
A type of body tissue that when contracted produces movement.

Organism
A living thing.

Ornithopod
A type of bird-hipped, plant-eating dinosaur that flourished in the Mesozoic Era, especially during the Cretaceous Period.

Pachycephalosaur
A bird-hipped dinosaur with a very thick skull.

Paleontologist
A scientist who uses fossil remains to study ancient animal and plant life.

Pangea
The single supercontinent that existed during the Triassic Period. It consisted of all the continents of the world fused together.

Panthalassa
The vast Triassic ocean that covered the part of the world not occupied by Pangea.

Plesiosaur
A Mesozoic marine reptile with either a long neck or long head and paddle-shaped limbs.

Predator
An animal that actively hunts other animals, known as prey, for food.

Preparator
A technician skilled in removing fossils from rock so that they can be studied by paleontologists.

"Prosauropod"
A lizard-hipped dinosaur that existed in the Triassic and early Jurassic Periods. It resembled a primitive type of sauropod.

Pterosaur
A flying reptile of the Mesozoic Era.

Pubis
One of the bones of the hip. In dinosaurs, it either stuck forward or was swept back. The classification of dinosaurs into bird- and lizard-hipped dinosaurs is based on the position of the pubis. In lizard-hipped dinosaurs, the pubis pointed forward, while in bird-hipped dinosaurs, it pointed backward.

Reconstruction
A skeleton of an extinct animal, built up from fossilized bones or casts made from the bones.

Restoration
A picture, film animation, or sculpture that shows how an extinct animal such as a dinosaur would have looked when it was alive.

Sandstone
A sedimentary rock made up of sand grains squashed together and then cemented by mineral deposits.

Sauropod
A lizard-hipped dinosaur. Sauropods were huge plant eaters that had long necks and walked on all fours.

Scavenger
An animal that feeds from the bodies of animals that are already dead.

Sediment
Material such as sand, mud, or silt that is deposited on the bed of a river or the ocean. When this undergoes diagenesis, it turns into sedimentary rock.

Stegosaur
A bird-hipped dinosaur with plates and spines on its back.

Supercontinent
A vast continent that consists of several continental landmasses fused together.

Taphonomy
The study of dead organisms before they become fossilized.

Tendon
The straplike tissue that attaches muscle to bones.

Theropod
A type of lizard-hipped dinosaur that walked on two legs. Many theropods were carnivores. This group eventually gave rise to birds.

Triassic Period
The first period of the Mesozoic Era, from 252 to 201 million years ago.

Vertebrate
An animal that has a backbone. The backbone, or spine, is made up of many individual bones, each one of which is called a vertebra.

INDEX

ACKNOWLEDGMENTS

The publisher would like to thank the following people for their help with making the book: Sam Atkinson, Kathakali Banerjee, and Rupa Rao for editorial assistance; Mary Sandberg for design assistance; Priyanka Bansal, Rakesh Kumar, Priyanka Sharma, and Saloni Singh for the jacket; Almudena Diaz, Nomazwe Mandonko, Jagtar Singh, and Vikram Singh for DTP assistance; Kate Humby and Caroline Stamps for proofreading; and Chris Bernstein for compiling the index.

Additional photography by:
Dave King, Andy Crawford, John Downes, Steve Gorton, Lynton Gardiner, Colin Keates, Harry Taylor, Jen and Des Bartlett and Gary Ombler.

Models made by:
Roby Braun, Jonathan Hateley, and Gary Staab.